The Million Dollar TFSA

How to Build a Tax-Free Fortune

Patrick Doucette

***

The Million Dollar TFSA

How to Build a Tax-Free Fortune

By

Patrick Doucette

Table of Contents

Preface

My average earnings within my TFSA (Tax Free Savings Account) have been over $4000 per month for the past twelve months running. How is this possible; especially when the Canadian government limits how much you can deposit into a TFSA each year?

Was it by taking crazy risk? Not really; I like to keep at least twenty percent of my account holdings in cash.

Was it by getting lucky on a single stock pick? Nope. Was it by trading constantly and thus turning my TFSA into a trading enterprise? No. Revenue Canada will likely tax you as a small business if you do that. It was by following simple, proven principles that I would like to share with you in this book.

Ask yourself, how much money would you need in a regular savings account to earn that much money? My bank currently offers me 0.1 % interest on my deposits. That's one-tenth of one percent interest. If I deposited one million dollars ($1,000,000) into a savings account with them, I would earn $1000 per year or about $83 per month. That is a very small amount; clearly, not enough to live on.

When you study the fine print; most Canadian banks offer interest under very restrictive conditions. They may offer you *some* interest but only if you don't touch the money for an extended period. You are unable to withdraw, no check writing, no debit payments, no bill payments and so on. Essentially you will currently earn little or no interest at all from most basic Canadian savings accounts. Checking accounts are even worse with monthly fees eating into your principal preventing you from earning any returns whatsoever.

But how does earning $10,610 dollars in a single month sound?[1] You could easily withdraw several thousand dollars and still grow your principal. Doesn't that seem like a great idea? You can build your TFSA into a small fortune that provides more income than if you held one million in cash. This book will fully explain how superior returns are possible for you and all Canadians who will take the time to be informed and implement these proven principles of wealth creation.

I'm not holding anything back; I will show what is possible in easy to follow steps that anyone can replicate for themselves. Let's examine these strategies together and start turning your TFSA from a savings account into a high yielding investing account.

Update January 17th, 2019

I would like to add an update because in this book, I mention a stock as an example of a good opportunity. As we have now discovered, a lot has changed since I first traded Aphria. I was in and out several times and finished with a net ten-fold return. I sold a good major chunk at $18.25 after witnessing a sudden drop in the selling price. Then after the short attack, I purchased some at $4.99 CDN and $5.18 CDN. Lastly, I sold my remaining shares at $9.00 CDN

It has been a long time since purchasing at a dollar and I am now relieved to be completely out of the stock. However successful the company may or may not be in the future, I could no longer in my conscious continue as a shareholder.

On a different note, I acquired a position in Trulieve, ticker symbol TRUL. I am also interested in WeedMD. Besides that, I am trying to keep a majority of my funds in cash due to the high valuations and associated risks.

I notice that some readers have complained that this book is too short so I will attempt to add updates as often as possible. I will keep my eye open for information that is not readily available elsewhere. I save a lot of things but most of it doesn't seem to provide much value.

Once thing I have learned is that I never rush to place a trade. I never trade from a position of anxiety or fear or greed. My intent is to come up with a plan and then stick to the plan. So, for example, with Trulieve, I saw that they announced a lockup on the shares, so I did not rush in to buy out of greed right away. I took some time to go over the financial data, look at their website and products. It is nothing difficult to go to Google maps and then search for dispensaries in Florida, I can see that they have good market coverage in the state. They appear to be the market leader, the state is announcing that they are finally going to allow flower sales so that should be a big boost to the revenue numbers over time, and so on and so forth. I do some of the things mentioned later in this book.

Once again, I try and examine it with fresh eyes and go through some possible scenario or projections and see what the potential market cap might be.

So currently their market cap is about $1.5 billion CDN, could that go to $15 billion? Well, yes hypothetically it could. They now have about 25 locations. Each location could do, say, 20 million in revenue down the road. That would be $500 million per year in revenue. (Now that may take a very long time but what if they add even more locations or expand to additional states) That would be a price to revenue multiple of 30 which is a little thick but of course it would depend on many other factors especially the net profit margin. But the thumbnail is not outlandish if the company is supportive of the shareholders and it seems that they are. So, I will invest on my end with good faith. I always invest from the point of view of a naive investor. I take what I read at face value and make the best decision I can. Because the market is changing so rapidly, my time horizon will likely be holding shares for only about a year. If the share price rises, I will plan to take some money off the table before the lock up expires, but if I believe in the company, it may be one that I would hold for several years.

Never give up and stay disciplined. I lot of my investment decisions turn out to be wrong, but I have the great advantage of being able to take action. I never fall in love with a stock; I stay objective. If I've made a mistake, I make a plan of how and when I am going to get out of a position. I always know what my stop loss is in my mind and even if it takes a few tries, I get into a position in a way that is 'comfortable' to my own trading or investing style.

The only other speculative company I would consider purchasing within my TFSA at the moment is WeedMD. Besides that, I am waiting for new opportunities and will stick to dividend stocks such as the Canadian Bank Stocks. I would like to thank you for purchasing this book and I hope it will help you and inspire you to invest wisely and to prosper in all things.

More updates to follow!

Update: February 3rd, 2020

I have initiated a position in the company WeedMD, ticker symbol WMD. Here is a brief analysis:

Speculations on WeedMD

Imagine that you are a syndicate. And by syndicate, I mean, a group of people that are excellent negotiators, highly motivated and looking to make a profit. They want to make a good living; they want to be good citizens and help people have jobs while earning a healthy income for their efforts.

Let's say this syndicate controls the union of construction workers in the province. They want to provide their workers cannabis as part of a benefits package. This helps those union members who suffer from chronic pain and many other ailments; many which are related to their difficult occupations in the construction industry.

They collect union dues from their workers and invest this money so that they can provide benefits and a pension to the workers when they retire.

They decide to take this money and buy shares in a company that produces cannabis. They invest $25 million in return for 94.9 million shares. This works out to a cost of about $0.26 cents a share. (26.3 cents) If we include an additional 17 million from a division (Starseed) we get a cost of $0.44 cents per share.

The market capitalization of the company goes from 125 million to 227 million instantly.

The number of shares outstanding goes from 116 million to 210.9 million.

If they received $25 million in cash. That would increase the deserved market capitalization from 125 million to 150 million. That would give a per share price of $0.71 cents.

The shares were $1.08. **They would need to drop to $0.71 cents to be equal to what they were before the issue of new shares for the $25 million.**

Does WeedMd get any other assets? They are listed at 50 million but let's just say they are zero. And the syndicate is losing $15 million per year.

Apparently, the syndicate includes an additional 17 million in cash. That would increase the deserved market capitalization to 167 million.

That would give a deserved share price of about **$0.79 cents per share.**

This deal gives them 45% of the shares. They only need to buy 5% more share in the open market. If their cost is $0.44 cents per share they can drive down the price and get the additional 5% of about 10.55 million shares for a cost of less than $10 million.

So now they own control of the company for their pension fund.

They have about 106 million shares maybe more at a cost about $0.50 cents per share or so.

They can try and drive the share price lower in the short term to get more shares cheaply. Then when they have over fifty percent ownership, they can start making profits. I would expect a share price drop between now and their next earnings release.

210.9 million share outstanding.

1 billion market cap = $4.74 per share.

5 billion market cap = $23.70 per share.

10 billion market cap = $44.74 per share.

This company is the ideal vehicle to channel cannabis supply to their union network. Outdoor grow for flower, concentrates, capsules etc.

Some other players could collapse.

WeedMD, the syndicate, could be one of the last men standing and be able to collect the shares of competitors for pennies.

Whether WeedMD shares bottom out at $0.71 or they may collapse to $0.44 cents in sympathy with the overall sector. I would buy at $0.79 and again at $0.44 if possible. Or buy at the current price and again at $1.00 on the way back up.

If you do not consider the losing $15 million per year. If this loss continues then the other option is to drive the company into the ground to zero and simply continue to supply through Starseed (out the backdoor) but this makes no sense as the motivation is to legitimize the business plan. I expect they would prefer to funnel profits into the pension plan legally to vindicate themselves as good citizens.

Best regards—Patrick Doucette   February 3, 2020

Introduction

As a Canadian you have an amazing opportunity to build wealth tax-free. Over eleven million Canadians now have a Tax-Free Savings Account. This is from a population base of about twenty-two million citizens that are between the age of 20 to 65. This tells us that about half of all Canadians between the ages of 20 and 65 have a TFSA.

Most Canadians know what a TFSA is; we all know that saving is a good idea. Yet, about 4.5 million people that opened a TFSA did not contribute in the last year. That means a full 40 percent of Canadians that have a TFSA, did not contribute in the past year! Only about 1.8 million Canadians max out their contributions each year. That means only 8 percent of eligible Canadians are taking full advantage of their TFSA.

This tells us that a lot of people like the idea of saving but are not committed. Many go to the trouble of opening their account but then never use it. In fact, almost a million Canadians closed their accounts in the past year![2]

Obviously, there are many who are unable to take advantage of a TFSA for many reasons. The purpose of this book is to help you, inspire you and guide you towards acting in the right direction. This book will give straightforward, diligent strategies that, if followed, will make you wealthy. There is information for both beginners and experienced investors.

There has never been a better time to secure a prosperous financial position for you and your loved ones. It does not take any special skills or abilities. All you need to do is follow the guidelines presented and slowly but surely, you will build wealth. Don't tell yourself it's too complicated or difficult. These ideas are available to every Canadian. Are you ready to build a tax-free fortune? Then let's get started!

Chapter 1 – The Groundwork

To begin the journey of building your TFSA into an income generating powerhouse, we need to cover some basic details. Sound financial management does not need to be difficult. The ideas presented will be easy to replicate by anyone that is able to hold a job. I would say by anyone that can fog a mirror; but you do need to have at least have some basic income. I built my TFSA from $10,000 to over $100,000 in just under two years on a very small income. In fact, my income was less than minimum wage while my TFSA was growing by leaps and bounds.

The Canadian government believes that it's a good thing for citizens to save a portion of their income. They know that if you build a nice nest egg in your TFSA, then they are less likely to have to pay for your expenses when you get older. They also know that you will eventually spend some of your earnings and we know they always get a cut when you spend. Whether you buy gas for your vehicle or fast food for your belly, the government always collects their cut.

To encourage the habit of saving, they created a form of savings account that allows you to earn returns within that account free from any tax. These earnings can be in the form of interest earned on your account balance, dividends paid on securities owned within your savings account, and capital appreciation realized on securities held within the account.

A TFSA is very similar to a self-directed RRSP except when you withdraw funds from an RRSP, you must declare it as income for the tax year in which it was withdrawn. Not so, in a TFSA. You can earn returns on your investments without the oppression of unnecessary tax. Finally, we have a situation where the government is really on your side! They want you to prosper using this unique and powerful investment strategy.

There is now little reason for anyone to open a self-directed RRSP. (Although you may still want an RRSP to reduce your income in a particular tax year.) A TFSA is the ultimate investment vehicle for all Canadians of legal age. You can deposit within your limits at any time without charge. You can also withdraw at any time without charge except if you withdraw, you cannot redeposit in the same taxation year without incurring a penalty.[3] You can purchase stocks within your TFSA and your bank will change you a modest commission. I pay $6.95 per trade at CIBC.

If you currently bank with one of the major Canadian banks, opening a TFSA is a very simple process. Simply contact your bank representative and place a request to open one. There is no fee and the paperwork amounts to your signature on a document or two. The main process of opening a TFSA can be done online. According to the

Canadian Bankers Association more than two thirds (68%) of Canadians do their banking digitally, using online and mobile banking.

Many people open a TFSA but then do not contribute anything into their account! Or if they do contribute, they simply leave the money as a cash deposit. Often, they are unaware that they can invest the money in their TFSA into a wide range of investments. Many contribute but then withdraw as soon as they face some unexpected day-to-day expenses. And as mentioned, many get discouraged for one reason or another and close their account due to their current financial needs.

Every working Canadian should open and maintain a TFSA if they ever hope to achieve a semblance of financial independence. The problem is that there is next to nothing in the form of marketing or promotion of this valuable investment option for Canadians. The media bombards us with messages telling us to spend. Spend on cars, trucks and food. Spend on vacations and sparkly jewelry. Spend on household furniture with free shipping. You get the idea. We are constantly reminded to do the opposite of what will benefit us the most.

To achieve financial independence requires a change in mindset from that of spending to that of **saving and investing**. If Canadians are continually trapped in 'spending mode' they will never break free from the cycle of personal debt and over-consumption; spending beyond our means. Spending beyond our means is a form of slow financial torture. **Decide now** not to be a slave to this way of living.

To begin, let's quickly look at the amounts that are allowable for TFSA contributions:

The TFSA program was started in 2009. From 2009 up to 2012 you could deposit $5000 per year. From 2013 to 2014 you could deposit $5500 per year. In 2015 the allowable contribution was raised to $10,000 for that year. And lastly, 2016 and 2017 you could deposit $5,500 per year.

The total amount you could have deposited since the program was started is $52,000. That is how much you would have in your account if you maxed out your contributions every year since it was started. These deposit amounts are cumulative. So, if you have never deposited any money into a TFSA yet, you could deposit $52,000 in one lump sum. Most people don't have 52 thousand dollars lying around so if you have not started yet, you have lots of room to contribute. You don't lose the ability to deposit if you skip a year; the allowable amount will just get rolled over into the next year. The Canadian government will also tell you on your Notice of Assessment how much contribution room you have available.

Here is a summary of the deposit amounts available:

Contribution room

Years	TFSA Annual Limit	Cumulative Total
2009-2012	$5,000	$20,000
2013-2014	$5,500	$31,000
2015	$10,000	$41,000
2016-2017	$5,500	$52,000

Now don't get discouraged out of the gate if you have not been saving these amounts. You are certainly not alone. Most Canadians are in the same boat, they are not able to max out their contribution room.

The average amount held in TFSA's by Canadians is just a little over $17,000.[4] Most Canadians are clearly not taking full advantage of their TFSA. They deposit some funds but then leave the money alone as 'dead money' or perhaps they might buy a mutual fund or two. Very few are willing to invest in a publicly traded company and some do not even realize that this is possible within their TFSA. Most Canadians have been lulled into a sense of learned helplessness. We are bombarded with messages telling us that it is too difficult or too risky to attempt any financial decisions on our own. When I say, "most Canadians" I am simply going by what the published statistics are indicating. The case will be different for you! Since you are reading this, it shows that you already have the energy and determination to break free from the crowd. You will break free from what the majority are doing.

It is important to keep in mind that there is no need to try and 'catch up' You can start depositing any time and you are only competing against yourself. Some may say, "Well it's too late for me now." No, it is not too late. You can start contributing any time you like. And of course, you can stop contributing (if you like) once you reach $10,000 in savings. I will cover how to save that first ten thousand in a later chapter. Ten thousand is a good number to start with. If you can save more, great; but I would recommend saving at least ten grand.

I was in the same boat as you. I looked at my contribution room a few years ago and was depressed. I saw these amounts on my Notice of Assessment and thought, "Well, thanks for telling me that I can contribute that much into my TFSA but how am I ever going to save that much when I am just scraping by?" The good news is that I only contributed a little over $10,000 and that was enough to get me started. I grew that $10,000 into over $100,000 in less than two years; 23 months to be exact; and if I did that, then so can you.[5]

I would like to take a moment to mention ETF's because they are so visible to investors these days. Many will choose to purchase mutual funds or ETF's (exchange traded funds). These investors will say, "I am happy to get 6% to 10% return on my investments on an annual basis." The problem is that we only have one lifetime. If you are happy with those types of return, then you don't need any suggestions to earn more. If you are reading this, then it suggests that you want to generate superior returns than the typical returns of mutual funds or Exchange Traded Funds.

My purpose is not to bash those types of investments. They are suitable for those persons who do not have the time or energy to take matters into their own hands. They would rather have someone else make their decisions for them. I will not go into details on ETF's because if you are reading this, it shows that you are looking for superior returns on your investments.

Now that you know how much you can deposit into your TFSA from the above table, we can move on to more important topics.

Chapter 2 – The Eighth Wonder of the World

Albert Einstein has been quoted as saying:

"Compound interest is the eighth wonder of the world. He who understands it, earns it...he who doesn't...pays it."

The understanding of compound returns is necessary for you to build your TFSA. We are going to assume that you have $10,000 saved up in your TFSA. Don't panic if you don't have that saved up yet; as mentioned, we will cover that in a later chapter.

You may have seen an explanation of compound interest that sounds like this: You deposit a certain amount per month, say $350 per month starting at age twenty and assuming a return of 6% interest per annum, you will have about one million dollars by the time you are age sixty-five. Isn't that just wonderful; but who does that?

If you start late, say at age 30, you would have to deposit about twice as much; about $700 per month to reach the same million dollars.

Let's start fresh and get all those low interest-bearing ideas out of your mind. First, how is any bank, financial institution, broker, wealth management company or anybody for that matter going to be able to give you a return on your deposits?

In theory, if you deposit your ten thousand dollars with a bank, they will give you one percent interest and then lend it out as mortgages and earn much higher interest; say three to six percent. The bank can even lend it out in the form of credit card debt at over twenty percent interest. Banks have lots of ways to make high interest and pay you very little on your deposits. This is a simplification of how Canadian banks make billions in profits.

What about wealth management companies? They also encourage you to give them your money and they promise a much higher return than the banks. In exchange for depositing your money with them, they will provide you with impressive statements every month about how your money is growing. But where do the returns come from? They claim that they will deposit your money in a diversified portfolio. What does a 'diversified portfolio' mean? Essentially it means spreading risk by investing in many different companies so that you are not, 'putting all your eggs in one basket'. The problem with this strategy is that you are simply following the 'crowd'. Examine the returns on the S&P 500 and you will see that the historical returns are not that great.

Let's assume that you take your initial ten thousand dollars that you have saved up and invest it in a single company that you believe will be successful. (Of course, you will not put all your funds into a single company; you need some diversification, but we will discuss that later.)

The company that you have chosen has a business plan that if executed successfully will see them grow by 35% per year. If this company can execute on their revenue growth plans, the value of that company as reflected in their market capitalization will normally also grow by a similar amount.

Example:

Let's say you buy 10,000 shares of a company at $1 (one dollar) per share. The company you have chosen has 100 million shares outstanding. Take the number of shares outstanding and multiply by the current stock price. This gives you the total value of the company.

In this simplified example, we see that the company is worth 100 million dollars. (100 million shares x $1 per share) = $100 million dollars.

By buying 10,000 shares, you are now part owner of that company. You now own 0.0001% of the company.

If the company succeeds in the marketplace, the share value will rise. Why will the share value rise? The share value will rise for multiple reasons. More people will want to be part owner of the company, so the share price will follow the actions of supply and demand. There will be more investors wanting to buy then there is investors willing to sell.

Second, the inherent value of the company will rise as their profits rise. Investors will start to be in a position of receiving dividends from the company. That is, if the company makes enough profit to cover all their expenses, whatever is left over may be distributed to the owners of the company in the form of cash payouts, i.e. dividends.

This is just theory as we know many companies never issue dividends; instead they re-invest any excess profits into growing the company.

Returning to our simple example; let's assume that the company has grown by 35% and the shares are now trading one year later at $1.35. The market capitalization of the company is now $135 million. Your initial investment is now worth $13,500. You have made (on paper) $3500.

What happens if the company grows at a similar rate for the next year?

The market capitalization at the end of year two has grown to $182.25 million. The shares at the end of year two are now trading at $1.82 and the value of your shares have grown to $18,200. The first year you earned $3500 but the second year you have earned $4,700.

Why is it, that in the first year you made $3,500 but in the second year you earned $4,700? This simple mathematical example shows the concept of compound returns. Without adding to your initial investment, you are making more. Interest on interest. Compound returns. Remember this simple concept.

Let's be more realistic. What if the company grows at only 10% per year. You hold your shares with the company for five years. What will the final year look like?

The company grows from a 100 million market cap to $161 million market cap. In the first year your investment grows by ten percent and you see a corresponding increase in the value of your investment of $1000. (10 percent of your initial ten thousand shares). In the fifth year, you would see an increase in your investment of $1,464. Do this calculation yourself and you will start to see the effect of compound returns.

Does this example also apply to interest returns from a bank? Yes, you can earn interest on interest but when you are dealing with a small interest rate, your returns take too long to be significant in your lifetime.

Remember the quote from Einstein at the beginning of this chapter and run a few examples yourself using different rates of return. This will help inspire you to take advantage of compound returns for yourself.

It took me over two years to save up $10,000 in my TFSA. It then took me another 23 months to grow my account from $10,000 to $95,000. But in a single day my account grew from $95,000 to $107,000! That is, my account grew 12.6% in a single day, giving me a return of over $12,000 in a single day. That is more than the original

$10,000 that took me two years to save up. Do you see the power of compound returns from this example?

These are the kind of returns you can get for yourself by being patient and diligent during the early years of saving and investing. You may start slow, but you can realize **exponential gains** if you stick with it and not give up.

Here is a table listing returns of 5%, 10% and 15% per period.

	5%	10%	15%
1	$10,500.00	$11,000.00	$11,500.00
2	$11,025.00	$12,100.00	$13,225.00
3	$11,576.00	$13,310.00	$15,208.00
4	$12,155.00	$14,641.00	$17,490.00
5	$12,762.00	$16,105.00	$20,113.00
6	$13,400.00	$17,715.00	$23,130.00
7	$14,071.00	$19,487.00	$26,600.00
8	$14,774.00	$21,435.00	$30,590.00
9	$15,513.00	$23,579.00	$35,178.00
10	$16,288.00	$25,937.00	$40,455.00
11	$17,103.00	$28,531.00	$46,523.00
12	$17,958.00	$31,384.00	$53,502.00

How long does it take to earn a 5% return on your investment? My average returns have been **12.35% per month** for the past two years. Most people would be happy to get 12.35% per year. Are there traders that can earn 12.35 % per week? Probably not. Yet I have already proven that over ten percent per month is possible. What rate of return will you be able to achieve? That is up to you.

Chapter 3 – Different Advice

Whether you have already opened a TFSA or are planning to; be aware that you will be presented with many offers to place your money somewhere else.

For example, I had an ad show up in my social media newsfeed that read, *"Nothing is riskier than trying to pick stocks."*

Now of course this company wants you to invest your money with them. And I don't want to knock anybody else. They are trying to help the public in their own way and I am trying to help the public with this book. There are probably lots of people that love their service. But, the ad states: *"Nothing is riskier that trying to pick stocks."* Do you think this statement is true? What about running through a forest barefoot? In winter. Or jumping out of an airplane without a parachute? That's probably a lot riskier.

So yes, the statement is false. There are a lot of things riskier than picking stocks. But they may argue that they are only talking about what you can do with your money. Okay.

I bet if you spend all your money on scratch lottery tickets, that would be quite risky. What if you fly to Las Vegas and place all your money down on the roulette wheel? I bet that would be riskier than picking stocks. Point made.

I have to hope that they provide a valuable service for many people that are unable to self-motivate.

I am obviously not a sophisticated investor. Yes, I have a have studied a little bit; but I am in the same boat as the next Canadian. Some things are hard to hide. If a company is taking on 1000 new clients per week; that should cause stir in anyone that has a mind for business.

Even the bank itself, while I was opening my TFSA encouraged me to put my deposits into a Guaranteed Investment Certificate. It is 'guaranteed' to provide me 1.75% interest if I promise not to touch it. So that $10,000 that I diligently saved will provide me $175 per year if I don't touch it. From that you would have to subtract any transfer fees, small print fees and other miscellaneous fees. Even without any extra fees subtract the current rate of inflation and you are earning a negligible amount; basically nothing. This is like loaning your money to someone at zero percent interest.

By the way, the small print reads, *terms and conditions apply.* Those terms and conditions lock in your money and force you to pay a penalty if you need to access your money prior to the end of the term. You can't blame the banks for doing this because they are in the business of making money for themselves. They are not concerned about making money for you; they want the better deal for themselves and that is another reason why Canadians banks make billions; that's billions with a 'B' every quarter.

Think about this for a moment, if I came up to you and said,

"Hey, can you lend me $10,000 for one year? I will pay you back at the end of a year. When I pay you back, I will give you an extra $175 bucks for your troubles but only if you meet all my hidden conditions. Otherwise I will give you back the $10,000 less my miscellaneous fees which will be calculated later."

Would you trust me or tell me to get lost? So why do many people choose to put their money into a GIC? Maybe because they just want to 'bury' their money and hopefully come back to it later. If you are reading this book, you have a much bigger vision for your financial destiny.

What about trusting your money to other 'wealth management' companies? There are many to choose from with distinguished names.

If you would like to trade your money for beautiful monthly statements and reassurances that all is well, then these are the type of companies to whom you could be handing over your money. They have excellent advisors who will gladly remove any financial responsibility from your mind.

Some claim, that nobody beats the market by picking stocks...really? Didn't a guy by the name of Warren Buffet do pretty good for himself? So, is that statement from such an ad true? No, again that is also a false statement. There are many Canadians who will pick stocks and beat the market. And by beat the market, I mean they will outperform the major indexes such as the S&P 500 or the Dow Jones Industrial Average.

A quick search tells me that the average annual return of the stock-market as a whole (using the S&P 500 index for a benchmark) is 11.69 %. That is better than the return from most mutual funds but that is still not great.

My returns within my TFSA have averaged 9.64% … **per month!** That is 116.00% percent per year; precisely ten times the return of the S&P 500! If those are my returns, there are likely many who take greater risk than myself and earn ever greater returns. That was over the past 24 months, so it has been a time of bull rush. There will no doubt be severe corrections.

There was nothing stopping someone from achieving similar results. I have had months with negative returns but those are my overall stats to date. You could do better or worse but even if did only half as well, you could still earn a healthy annual return on your money; a return that is far better than what you would get by giving away your money to someone else to manage for you.

I am not an insider; I do not have any special talent for picking stocks and I pick stocks based on very simple criteria. Therefore, there are likely many investors who fare much better than myself. I don't know who the first Canadian will be to grow their TFSA to one million dollars. I hope it is me; maybe it will be you; but I would bet good money that it will not be by someone who hands over their savings to a wealth management company to be put into mutual funds or ETF's.

If you are reading this, it is an indicator that you are willing to take matters into your own hands. You will not be taken in by these alluring advertisements to get your hard-earned money. You deserve better than that. This is one of the most important areas of life in which you still have the freedom to take control: in your own personal finances.

As a citizen of the economic system in which we live, I see it as my duty to manage my finances with diligence and prudence. To ignore that responsibility with excuses would be at my own economic peril. I choose to take control of my money and so should you. Take control of your money. Think of your TFSA deposits as liquid capital; real money that has the power to make you more money. Once you give away your money you are no longer in the game.

Don't believe the advertisements. You will see paid actors making statements like this:

"I'm good at saving, but I am hopeless at investing."

"I can make money and spend it, but I don't have a clue about the stock market."

"I trust my financial advisor; they are the best at what they do."

It's time to **believe in yourself**. Trust yourself with your own money.

Once you have made the decision to take control of your financial destiny you need information to make the right choices in the money marketplace. And that brings us to the next chapter.

Chapter 4 – Catch the Right Train

Before I talk about choosing specific investments, I would like to ask you a question. If you had to choose the top three trends of today, what would they be? The internet? Smart Phones? Electric Cars? You may have different choices. As an investor you want to look around and see what is growing and then match that up with what you have first hand knowledge on.

Maybe you think one the top three trends is the internet and you see that the company you work for is choosing Shopify to handle their online presence. You do a little digging and you find out that Shopify is handling a lot of different companies these days. Wouldn't that make you want to be an investor in that company?

But then you do a little research and you discover that they have a market capitalization of 10 Billion dollars already and are not turning a profit yet. You decide to keep looking.

What about electric cars. Maybe you just bought a Tesla and you love it. Or maybe you hate it and traded it in for a Chevy Volt! What electric car do you think is the best? Does that electric car company have the potential to grow its sales by over thirty percent per year? You get the idea of some of the questions you need to ask.

Never worry that you have missed the train. Forest Gump was released in 1994 and there is a point in the movie where Forest finds out that his friend had invested his money in some kind of "fruit company". We watch as Forest opens a shareholder letter and the company is Apple Computer. We laughed at that scene because we all know what a success story Apple *was*...in 1994! Imagine if you had invested in Apple long after Forest; you would still have earned an impressive return on your investment.

Maybe you think a big trend is none of the above; maybe you think Yoga is the biggest thing. Why not look at Lulumon? You discover they already have a market capitalization of 10 billion but they have earnings of $2 per share.

If you use their products, then look at their sales forecast and invest accordingly. There will always be new companies that have the potential to grow at over 30% per year in market capitalization and those are the companies you want to be invested in.

Don't try and get on a train that is *not* going in the direction you want to travel! You want to be on a train that is going in the right direction; and that is growing. Don't look for a turnaround. These are tempting because we like to be contrarian, we like to pick bottoms. Don't try and pick bottoms; pick a company that is already succeeding and just continue with that success. It can be mentally difficult to buy a stock that "is already high". But that simply means it has a greater likelihood of going higher. Yes, there are exceptions, but I think you get the idea. Catch a winning train, not a train that is stopped nor a train that is going in the wrong direction.

Sometimes an investor feels that they must have a secret "stock tip" that no one else knows about. Don't think that way. If the stock is valuable, many people will know about it. If a stock is a secret, stay away from it! If it is a large powerful moving train, then jump on board; like an Apple or a Lululemon for instance. You will have more gains this way than from the secret stock tip or from trying to pick a rebounder.

There is currently a train that about to leave the station and maybe you want to call it a secret, but it is a secret in plain sight. That secret is the legalization of cannabis. Canadian companies will have a head-start because the government has already approved legislation that will see cannabis being legalized nationwide on July 1st, 2018.

The leading companies in this space are **Canopy Growth Corporation** (ticker symbol: weed, market capitalization of about 3 billion), **Aurora Cannabis** (ticker symbol: acb, market capitalization of about 2.5 billion, and **Aphria Inc** (ticker symbol aph, market capitalization of about 2 billion.

My easy choice of the three is Aphria because they are the lowest cost producer, they wholesale to other licensed producers. Ask the question, will they eventually have a market capitalization of ten billion dollars like shopify and lululemon? The answer is a simple, Yes!

I excluded Aurora because I did not understand their financing deals. I excuded Canopy because I thought they were wasting money. (that was an error on my part!). **Looking back in retrospect it is amazing that I got out of that decision in one piece!**

Besides these three, there are dozens of more players that are a bit late to the market yet still have the potential to be profitable companies. There are dozens more that are just an idea or a pitch that you want to avoid. It is not difficult to avoid those ones by using common sense.

Put some of your TFSA investment into Aphria and you will be getting on board a large freight train that is moving in the direction of profitability.

(Update: Maybe let's not do that after all! I would consider TRUL, TRST, HEXO. I exited my remaining position in Aphria in January, 2019.

Chapter 5 – Information Sources

After you have opened a TFSA and have been diligently contributing, you are now ready to choose investments. Ideally you have saved up $10,000 but you can begin your investing decisions at any time. Remember that a TFSA is not just a savings account, think of it more as an investment account like a self-directed RRSP. The difference being that you can earn income within your TFSA and not be taxed on the gains that accrue within or when withdrawn; that is, if you follow the rules provided by the CRA (Canada Revenue Agency). Since you are depositing after tax dollars, all your gains will be free and clear of the tax-man.

The Canadian Government provides a list of stock exchanges that qualify as acceptable investments within your TFSA. I have highlighted the exchanges that you will most likely be interested in:

Canada: Aequitas NEO Exchange

Canada: **Canadian National Stock Exchange (operating as the Canadian Securities Exchange) (CSE)**

Canada: Montreal Exchange

Canada: **TSX Venture Exchange (Tiers 1 and 2)**

Canada: **Toronto Stock Exchange**

Australia: Australian Securities Exchange

Austria: Vienna Stock Exchange

Belgium: Euronext Brussels

Bermuda: Bermuda Stock Exchange

Brazil: BM&F Bovespa Stock Exchange

Czech Republic: Prague Stock Exchange (Prime Market)

Denmark: Copenhagen Stock Exchange

Finland: Helsinki Stock Exchange

France: Euronext Paris

Germany: Frankfurt Stock Exchange

Germany: Boerse Stuttgart AG (Stuttgart Stock Exchange)

Hong Kong: The Hong Kong Stock Exchange

Ireland: Irish Stock Exchange

Israel: Tel Aviv Stock Exchange

Italy: Milan Stock Exchange

Jamaica: Jamaica Stock Exchange (Senior Market)

Japan: Tokyo Stock Exchange

Luxembourg: Luxembourg Stock Exchange

Mexico: Mexico City Stock Exchange

Netherlands: Euronext Amsterdam

New Zealand: New Zealand Stock Exchange

Norway: Oslo Stock Exchange

Poland: The main and parallel markets of the Warsaw Stock Exchange

Republic of Korea: Korea Exchange (KOSPI and KOSDAQ)

Singapore: Singapore Stock Exchange

South Africa: Johannesburg Stock Exchange

Spain: Madrid Stock Exchange

Sweden: Stockholm Stock Exchange

Switzerland: SWX Swiss Exchange

United Kingdom: London Stock Exchange

United States: BATS Exchange

United States: Boston Stock Exchange

United States: Chicago Board of Options

United States: Chicago Board of Trade

United States: Chicago Stock Exchange

United States: **National Association of Securities Dealers Automated Quotation System (NASDAQ)**

United States: National Stock Exchange

United States: **New York Stock Exchange (NYSE)**

United States: NYSE Arca

United States: NYSE MKT

United States: Philadelphia Stock Exchange

You can see that there are many stock exchange options for the TFSA holder.

When investing in a public company by buying their shares, you are becoming a part owner of that company. This is the mindset you should have. You want to base your decision on whether to invest or not on the most accurate information that is available.

If the company is offering a new technology, you want to be a customer of that new technology if possible. That will allow you to see first-hand whether you believe the company will prosper in the long run. If the company is providing retail goods, you want to see what kind of service they are providing. Whenever possible, you want to decide based on your own experience rather than on second-hand data.

If you see a new retail location open in your neighborhood, take the time to visit. Maybe it is a lululemon athletica store, maybe it is a new restaurant.

As an investor I am currently interested in the Cannabis sector and that is how I have been able to grow my TFSA from 10k to over 100k in a relatively short period of time. Now you may be totally opposed to this sector for personal reasons but don't let that stop you from benefiting from the strategies mentioned below. These strategies are applicable to all sectors. It's about doing a little bit of homework and a little bit of digging for information that is available to everyone.

Customer Newsletters

Since I am currently interested in the Cannabis sector. I sign up for each of the customer newsletters from the major licensed producers. How hard is it to compare what each of them are offering? What company do I feel is offering the best deals? Most customers will be on the mailing list of their own supplier but there is nothing stopping you from signing us for every newsletter. It's free and only takes a moment of your time. If you are worried about getting too many emails, just set up a dedicated email account for this purpose.

As a potential investor, it is not difficult to see that Cannabis stocks are currently 'hot' as opposed to say, stocks in the oil and gas industry that are currently slumping. Although I am writing this in late 2017, you could apply this to any industry for which you have interest.

For any company that I am considering investing in, the first thing I do is sign up for their free newsletter if they have one. These will provide updates as to their product offerings, availability and pricing. I can compare these and see how they stack up in relation to one another.

Trade Shows

Attending trade shows are an excellent way of getting first-hand information on the companies you are interested in becoming a part owner. Look at the company's booth setup. Speak to the representatives, get their card and ask them how they enjoy working for the company. Do they sound excited and motivated to present their pitch to you?

I attended a cannabis trade show in Toronto a couple of years back and this helped me to decide to invest in Aphria when it was in the $1 to 2$ per share range. The employees that were representing them were motivated and eager to answer my questions as an investor. They had a fly-over video of their greenhouses that were under construction.

Take advantage of any business to business tradeshows that are in the sector of your own interest. The information you gain can result in big dividends. And don't be shy about representing yourself as an investor. Whether you can purchase 100 shares or 100,000 shares; every investor is important to companies that are in the early stages of growth. Dress the part and prepare your questions thoughtfully. Don't try and get 'insider information' and don't be bothersome yet be willing to ask some pointed thoughtful questions. For example:

How are they attracting new customers? What makes them better than their competitors? Are they currently hiring and for what positions?

That last question is very important. Notice what positions they are looking to fill and keep a mental note in comparison to their competitors.

Sedar Files

Public companies are required to regularly submit documents to the exchange they are listed on. These documents are made available to the public at **www.sedar.com**. Of interest are the Management Discussion and Analysis files. Read through these as best you can. Does it take time and effort? Yes, but it is worth every moment of your time.

There are also financial statements of various types. Sometimes these documents are difficult to understand especially when they start talking about options, warrants, convertible debentures and who knows what. I confess that I am not a Finance major nor am I an accountant. The Management Discussion and Analysis (MD&A) along with an income statment is usually enough to give me a decent idea of what is going on.

I like to know the basic details: How many shares are outstanding? How much revenue is the company making? What is their projected revenue? How many shares do the principals of the company own?

As you get your feet wet in investing, you can ask tougher questions. Who are the directors of the company? How are they paid? Will the shares be diluted in the future when the company tries to raise more money? Will the company need to issue more shares? Have the owners of the company been selling their own shares?

As your knowledge grows, you will get more comfortable in going over the financial statements that are published by each company every quarter.

Conference Calls

Many public companies will host a conference call to discuss their latest results. This usually takes place immediately after quarterly results are posted. Sometimes these calls are restricted but often they are open to anyone that wants to listen in. They are also usually recorded for playback later. This will give you a good feel for how management responds to questions from their shareholders.

Press Releases and Print Media

Keep in mind that press releases, newspaper coverage and television coverage are old news. That is, the news has usually already been factored into the price of the stock. If you are following a buy and hold strategy, then these news reports should act as a confirmation of the research that you have done weeks or months before. You don't want to trade based on old news. 'Buy on rumor and sell on fact' is a phrase that traders use; however, that maxim is more for the short-term trader. Ideally you will want to be a buy-and-hold investor to realize the best gains - Warren Buffet style!

YouTube Videos

Switching from conventional sources of information we see an unexpected source for information; YouTube videos.

Sometimes at a trade show or at a private investor presentation, a presentation is recorded on video and then uploaded to the internet. Since you cannot attend every trade show or investor presentation. Search the company name you are considering on YouTube and see what comes up. Often you will get up to date data from this popular site.

Social Media Presence

As an investor you want to keep your eyes and ears open to any unconventional sources of information. What is the company's Facebook page look like? Do they post honest feedback from clients or is their page curated and filtered? Do they keep clients up to date with twitter posts? Do they encourage direct feedback from their customers and shareholders? You may find support groups that are not directly related to the company you are interested in; these can also be helpful in making your decision as an investor.

You have to gain a sense for 'mis-information'. And for that I mean you don't want to chase a stock just because you heard about it on social media. Even though it is difficult to get first-hand information, you should make best attempts at some kind of due diligence. Realize the risks you are taking.

The key to all these sources of information is that you are actively listening with an open mind. If you close your mind to learning and listening, then you are straight back with those investment advisors who will gladly do your investment thinking for you. Take charge of your own money and never let anyone make the decisions that only you should be making. This will save you much regret and help you prosper beyond what you may have thought possible.

Chapter 6 – A Threefold Cord

After I have summarized my own direct research, I am ready to choose my investments. The wise King Solomon once said, *"A threefold cord is not quickly broken."*[6] I currently decide to take 80% of my TFSA balance and divide it into three different stocks and hold 20% in cash.

Is this a risky strategy? Yes. It would be much better to follow Solomon's other piece of advice: *"Give a portion to seven, and also to eight; for thou knowest not what evil shall be upon the Earth."*[7]

So even though I know I should diversify more, each investor has their own trading style and temperament. You may choose a single company to invest or you may choose seven or eight in keeping with Solomon's advice. This can only be determined by yourself. More important is to get your money in the game. Don't just hold cash. Get your feet wet and choose a company that is your favorite. Over time you will discover your own disposition towards investing and adapt accordingly.

Don't be afraid of trying to pick a winner. Do you have a favorite sports team? Do you cheer for seven or eight different teams or do you have just one favorite?

When I first started investing within my TFSA; with my initial ten thousand, I picked a single stock. Even though this is considered a foolish strategy, I followed my own gut instincts which paid off. Later, I diversified into these three: Aphria (APH), Canopy Growth Corp (WEED) and Organigram (OGI). This is the sector I was most familiar with. You may do the same in a specific industry. Bet on the top three and then watch to see which performs the best.

In my case, over time, I sold all my stock in Organigram because they unfortunately faced a lawsuit. Since I had no idea how that could impact their earnings in the future I decided to get out with a nice profit.

This is the beauty of the stock market. Where else can you become part owner of a company yet if things go sour, you can simply jettison all ties to the company by selling your shares? Small business owners and most entrepreneurs are tied to their own company. You have more freedom as an investor than the management of most companies. Use that freedom to your advantage.

Later I sold my shares in Canopy which was trading under the name Tweed at the time. Why did I sell? Several reasons. I visited a trade show in Toronto and had a chance to speak to representatives from many different companies. At the show Tweed was providing free lattés and cappuccinos to the attendees. My parsimonious mind was asking myself, "As part owner of the company, would I want to buy free coffees for everyone?" That must have cost around several thousand dollars, even though that is a spit amount; it made me pause. I guess I just felt the company was spending too much on sales & marketing and not enough on infrastructure.

Second as a customer, I noticed that the prices for their product was not quite as competitive as some other licensed producers even though they were very close. And lastly, I noticed that their website was down for several days in the spring of 2017. I realize how devastating this can be to a company's goodwill and sales. I just felt that they were a bit too free-wheeling when it came to spending money. Were these good reasons to sell? Well in hindsight I was probably wrong to sell. Canopy shares went on to soar quite nicely so yes, I guess you could say I was wrong.

But the important thing was that I made the best decision I could using the information that was available to me at that time. No regrets.

My goal is always to base my trading decisions on as many facts as I can gather. I don't try and get 'inside' information. That's the last thing you need; that will only get you in trouble. The information you need is available for all to see. Check the Sedar documents, read as much as you can, both from the company and from their competitors. Then, and only then, follow your gut. Don't be afraid of making a mistake.

One reason I never bought any stock in Aurora Cannabis (ACB) is that I could not understand their financing deals. They had warrants and options up the wahzoo; I could not make head nor tail of what they were doing. I may have made a mistake by not buying their shares just like I did on Tweed but that did not stop me from investing in companies that I could better understand.

Go with what gives you confidence. When you invest in a company, you should be proud of that company. It should not seem murky or mysterious. Ask the basic questions. These I consider my three golden questions:

1. **How many shares are outstanding?**
2. **What is the total market capitalization of the company?**

3. **What are the expected earnings?**

That last general question you might call the 'platinum question' because that will give you the expected earnings per share, the P/E (Price to Earnings) Ratio and the EBITDA (Earnings before interest taxes and depreciation and amortization.)

As you become familiar with these numbers, you will gain greater confidence in your own investing decisions. Don't worry if you do not understand at first. With a little patience and experience you will realize that as earnings grow, profits grow, and the share price goes up. It doesn't get any simpler than that. Those are the companies you want to invest in. Companies that are growing their earnings and net profits. That's where the smart money will go and that is where you want to invest; in winning companies! Pick the winners.

Don't be a contrarian.

A lot of beginner investors like the idea of being a contrarian. They have heard 'somewhere' that it is a good thing to be a contrarian, so they are always looking for a stock to turn around after it has been in a downtrend for some time. Even though we are in the midst of a tidal wave of money being poured into the cannabis sector; many would rather pick a stock in the oil and gas or retail sector. For some reason people just feel better trying to pick a bottom. Don't do that.

'The trend is your friend.' Think of the stock price as a bus that can take you to profits. If the stock is going up, that's the same direction you want to be going. You wouldn't jump on a bus that is going in the opposite direction of your destination. The same is true for stocks. And that brings us to the topic for the next chapter on timing.

Chapter 7 – Timing

When is it a good time to buy? There are some people that evaluate a stock based only on its' current share price. They consider a stock a good deal if it is trading for less than a dollar and consider it 'expensive' if it is trading for say, above $50 per share. Evaluating a company simply on its current share price is clearly incorrect. Yet, many uninformed Canadians still think this way.

There are a few basic questions you can ask to help to know whether a stock is a good deal or not.

How much gross revenue do I believe this company can earn? How much net income do I believe this company can earn? What is the current price to earnings ratio (P/E Ratio) and what will it be one year from now? What is the P/E ratio for companies in the same business category? What is the market capitalization of this company? If the company hits their revenue target, what would I expect the market capitalization to be?

When I was much younger I was eager to time the market based on technical analysis. I would make all sorts of charts attempting to buy low and sell high. Now that I am older, and hopefully wiser, I do not depend on this method that much. I still try sometimes as old habits die hard, but I do with a small amount of my investment funds.

It is possible to think of timing the market in a different light. Imagine you go into business with a friend and you open a coffee shop together. Your business grows quickly, and you begin to make a profit. But suddenly you decide to just leave. You don't show up for work one day and your partner is left alone. You take an extended holiday without telling him. The business suffers, and profits drop. Then you reappear and decide to join him again. What would you think of such a partner?

Isn't that a bit like timing the market? The price of your investment goes up, so you try and cash out without regard to others. The stock market is the only place where it is legal to try to steal from one another! Each is trying to take advantage of the greed of the other. Shareholders are trying to squeeze every penny they can out of their investments and the management is trying to squeeze as much compensation as they can from their shareholders!

Or perhaps it is better to think of investing as planting your seeds. Your money is your seed that you plant in the ground. If you pull them up at the first sign of green, you will never enjoy the real fruit of long-term capital appreciation, let alone the possible dividends and stock splits that take a long time to mature.

Even though I know that buying and holding is the correct strategy and it seems, some might argue, to be a, 'morally superior' strategy, I still try and time the market with a small amount of capital while keeping the bulk of my investment going towards my long-term goals. I do this because it is fun and, I confess, because it feeds the ego.

The best time to take a position in a company is the same day that you have completed your research. Technical analysis made me become a slave to my charts. I would look at one-minute charts, 15-minutes, hourly, daily; you get the idea. It was all candlesticks and spinning tops and overbought this or oversold that! This caused me to waste far too much time in front of my computer.

I confess I am still a bit hooked on charts, but I no longer try and jump in and out as much as I did when I was younger.

The way I look at it now. I've done my research and I take a position. The price goes up, great! All smiles! But then the greed kicks in and I am tempted to lock in my profit by selling. That might be like going to work for a company but as soon as I see the company doing well, I decide to not go to work anymore. What kind of partner am I if I quit as soon as I see the stock go up?

Warren Buffet has already proved that buy and hold is the way to go. Unless I find some genuine fundamental reason for selling. Like the example with Organigram and their lawsuit. Maybe they can settle all the claims for a few million dollars but what if it is a much higher settlement?

The same was with Canopy, I sold based on facts that I observed. Even though I was clearly 'wrong' in selling; I made the decision to sell based on several facts and not just based on my own greed. By selling my shares, I was able to choose an alternate.

Aphria became my number one holding and I have no plans to jump ship just because they are doing well. There will be plenty of opportunity to sell down the road. My time frame for selling would be measured in years, not weeks or months. My long-term vision would be for a stock split or to be able to earn a dividend payout on my shares; sharing in the profits of the company.

I have not abandoned technical analysis altogether. I still find that oversold indicators can be helpful when looking for an entry point. For example:

In the above image you can see that the price has been in a down trend from mid-April until June 5th. I noticed that the stochastic and Williams %R indicators are coming off their lows. That is, the price of the stock is making new lows, but the technical indicators are not. I was able to place a buy order the following day and was filled at $4.75 CDN per share.

The share price subsequently rose as shown in the image below:

At this point I could have taken profits if I wanted. This is a common strategy, in one form or another, for many traders. So even though I prefer a buy and hold strategy; technical analysis can sometimes be helpful in deciding when to pull the trigger on your short-term trades.

Having spent many fruitless hours trying to develop a trading system based on technical analysis alone, I confess to you that I have abandoned that method. Some traders swear by their candlestick indicators and some are very successful with their 'swing trading methods'; good on them. I will not knock someone else's methods of trading. My choice is long-term hold using months or years as a time frame and not days or weeks. I expect that as cannabis legalization begins to take hold, we will see healthy profits for those companies that are able to execute on their business plans just as in any industry.

If you have no interest in the cannabis sector, ask yourself what industry are you interested in? What is your favorite retail product? Is it clothing like Canada Goose or technology like Apple or Shopify or Blackberry? Find a company that you are excited about and that you would like to be a part owner. That is really the best motivation for investing your hard-earned after-tax dollars.

Purchase shares in a company that has already started to be successful and is earning profits. If they do not have net income; that is income after all their expenses, giving them some positive earnings per share; it is probably too early to invest in that company. Of course, there are exceptions to every rule, but this general idea is sensible.

If you are aghast at any type of risk, why not buy shares in the major Canadian banks. Even if their share prices fluctuate a lot, you will still earn regular dividends on your investment. By investing in

Canadian bank stocks, you will fare better than any GIC and better than most mutual funds.

Chapter 8 – Running the Numbers

Think of the current market capitalization of the largest companies. Apple, 898 billion, Amazon 571 Billion, General Electric 157 billion and so on. Market capitalization is the price of the shares multiplied by the number of shares outstanding. This number is important to you as an investor. Why is it so important? Because that is the number you will use for the future projection of the share price of the stocks in which you have interest.

The price to earnings of Apple is about 20. The price to earnings for General Electric is about 22. The price to earnings for Amazon is about 300. Why is the price to earnings for Amazon so high? It is likely because the market believes that future earnings will increase dramatically.

I look at the companies that I am interested in as a potential investor. I will use Aphria (APH) as an example. I see that Aphria is currently trading at about $10 per share with a market cap of 1.5 billion. The market cap is simply the number of shares outstanding multiplied by the share price. That's simple math; there are about 150 million shares outstanding. If you can multiply $10 x 150 million, you get the market cap of 1.5 billion.

Why do so many people claim that they are not good with money or that they don't have a mind for investing? It just seems to be a strange aspect of human nature. It could be based on hidden fears. Who knows? But you will see so many celebrities, professional athletes, and others who will claim they are successful in one area of their life, but then they can't manage their money. They abdicate, they throw away their own opportunity to build lasting wealth for themselves and those they care about.

If you can do simple math and look around and see what is happening, then you can invest your own funds. Back to the example of market capitalization.

As already mentioned, Aphria is currently trading at $10 per share (as of November 2017) with a market cap of 1.5 billion. (That is the current share price of $10 multiplied by the number of shares issued which is about 150 million). I ask the question, will this company ever reach a market cap of say, 10 billion dollars? How much revenue would the company have to earn for the market to value it at 10 billion? That is, how much would the company have to earn for the market capitalization to reach 10 billion?

Aphria is quite vocal about their plan to produce 100,000 kgs of cannabis per year within a couple of years. That equals 100 million grams. (simple math again; 1 kilogram = 1000 grams) If average selling price is $7.50 per gram, that means they can hope to achieve $750 million dollars in gross revenue.

If they achieve $750 million in gross revenue, what would be the net earnings? That is the 'E' part of the P/E ratio. Well, selling cannabis has good margins; their cost to grow is about a buck a gram. After all their selling costs like marketing, salaries, overhead and so on; we could expect a net income of at least 30% of gross revenue. That would give us $225 million in net income.

Next, we ask ourselves, what is the average P/E ratio of their industry? They currently trade at 60 times earnings. Let's be more conservative and estimate a P/E ratio of 25 times earnings. This is an average P/E ratio of companies in the same or similar biotech/healthcare/cannabis sector.

225 million x 25 = 5.625 billion

A market cap of 5.625 billion should be achievable in the marketplace within a couple of years if they achieve their revenue target. So now you must test your math skill as an educated investor! If we believe that they can produce and sell that much product what would be the expected price of their shares in the marketplace?

It is a simple calculation. The market capitalization of 5.25 billion divided by the number of shares outstanding which is about 150 million.

5.625 billion = 5,625 million / 150 million = **$37.50 per share.**

What would the selling price of the stock be if the P/E ratio remained at 60? First, we should ask if such a P/E ratio is sustainable? Maybe, maybe not; that number would depend on their outlook at that time in the future. To compare I will calculate the share price with a P/E ratio of 40 and a P/E ratio of 60.

P/E Ratio of 40 =

Projected net income of 225 million x 40 = market cap of 9,000 million (9 billion)

9 billion divided by 150 million shares outstanding = **$60.00 per share**.

P/E Ratio of 60 =

Projected net income of 225 million x 60 = market cap of 13.5 billion

13.5 billion / 150 million shares = **$90.00 per share**.

These are the simple math exercises you should be able to calculate when thinking of the future value of the stock.

What happens if the company issues more shares? Does this dilute the value of the shares? That depends on what they do with the money they raise. Let's say they issue another 50 million shares but do not increase revenue.

From our first example:

5.625 billion / 200 million shares gives a projected share price of **$28.12**. This is much less than our first projection of **$37.50** per share. If the issuance of new shares allows them to increase revenue, this will offset the expected dilution as shown in the above example. For example, if they use the money raised to increase earnings to 300 million, the expected share price target will not change:

300 million x P/E ratio of 25 = market capitalization of 7.5 billion.

7,500 million / 200 million shares = **$37.50**

Raising money by issuing shares will dilute the potential profits if the money that is raised is <u>wasted</u>. But if the money raised can increase net income, this will offset the dilution.

If you are drawing a blank on this chapter, don't panic. There are plenty of resources that can help you understand the basic terms. You should try and familiarize yourself with the following terms: the **price earnings ratio**, **market capitalization** and **earning per share.**

If you can follow these simple calculations, then you are already ahead of the pack. You can pat yourself on the back and then continue to study more detailed aspects of the industry in which you have an interest. Basic accounting skills that allow you to read an income statement are not difficult to learn.

Having a predetermined share price target will allow you to escape from micro-managing your funds. That is, it will help prevent you from over-trading on each rise and fall of the share price. Stocks in emerging sectors, like the cannabis industry will naturally have wild swings in response to market developments. By having a firm price target, you can buy and hold until you have strong evidence to do otherwise. Personally, I would like to hold Aphria until it reaches $90 per share while continuing to monitor the price earnings ratio. Then re-examine the company in relation to new products offered, what their competitors are doing and so on and so forth. This type of analysis is very straightforward and understandable by anyone with an interest and the patience to employ a reasonable amount of study.

Remember that quote from Henry Ford: "*Whether you think you can or whether you think you can't; you are right.*" Believe that you *can* become an educated investor and you *will* become an educated investor. This book is just a taste. You are just dipping your foot in the ocean; but it is an ocean of money from which you can draw! Read the book, **Beating the Street** by **Peter Lynch**. That is what got me started. My hope is that this book will be just a start for you as well; as you learn more and more every day. You can do it, just as I did!

Chapter 9 – Escape from the Lies

Continuing with the example from the previous chapter. If we expect the future value of Aphria shares to be $90 per share within say, three years and the price is currently $10 per share, why don't most Canadians buy as many shares as they can? Because they are already spending most of their money on housing and automobiles!

Do you see any commercials on television, radio or on the web, telling you to buy shares in Canadian public companies? No, of course not. But you see a lot of commercials telling you to buy the new latest pick-up truck.

Arlene Dickinson, one of the most visible Canadian entrepreneurs was a director for Aphria for a short while. That barely made a single news headline. Think about that for a moment; one of the most well-known and respected Canadian entrepreneurs gave of her time and expertise in a new Canadian venture that most people are still wondering whether it is a legitimate investment.

If you can understand chapter eight, then you can break out of the lies that have kept you from being a successful investor. I often ask people in they have any interest in investing. These are some the answers I have heard.

"I have some money with xyz & company. I get about 6 to 10 percent return per year. Never less that 6% and I am totally happy with that."

"Investing is too risky. I don't like risk."

"I would if I had any money."

"I'm not a trader. I don't want to stare at a screen all day."

"I'm too impatient."

"Investing in stocks, are you kidding? You may as well just shoot darts at a dartboard."

"That's a scam."

"That's just gambling."

"For every buyer, there is a seller. It's a zero-sum game so if you are investing in stocks, it's like trying to steal from someone else."

Why should you let yourself be lulled into a state of helplessness? The media has little interest in educating us. They only want us to buy their product.

What about your close family members; will they help you to become wealthy? The only thing my dad ever told me was to get a job. I can still hear him telling me, "You may as well just throw your money in the stock-market." No offense to my dad but he made that statement with such a tone of contempt that it was clear he considered anything to do with the stock-market to be on the same level as playing craps in Vegas.

What if my dad or his dad had just put a few thousand dollars in a few public companies. My life would be different. I probably would have gone to better schools. I probably would not have fought and struggled so much as a kid. My dad, God bless him, he worked hard his entire life. Nobody ever told him anything about investing. Just as he never told me anything about investing.

How many people buy a new car each year in Canada? Here is some data from Statistics Canada:

New Motor Vehicle Sales in Canada			August Sales	September 2017 projected
Total Sales			187,257	190,581
Passenger Cars			60,862	58,817
North Amercan			39,237	38,141
Overseas/Imports			21,625	20,676
Trucks			126,395	131,764

Over 190,000 new vehicles sold in the month of September 2017 alone! The automotive companies are having a banner year and Canadians are sinking further and further into debt. We are wasting our money on depreciating assets like cars, trucks, clothing, and jewelry. This is not to mention the money spent on cellphones and food!

Over two million Canadians will buy a new vehicle this year and about one million will close their TFSA! What is wrong with this picture? Canadians are being bombarded with the message to spend, spend and spend some more. They are building themselves into a debt position that keeps them a slave to theirs jobs. You know what a job is? That's right; J-O-B = Just Over Broke!

If those same Canadians bought a second-hand vehicle and invested those monthly payments instead into companies that are producing products for international export; we would be the richest country in the world!

Don't be a Baby Elephant!

Have you heard the story about how they train baby elephants? I was lucky enough to see Brian Tracy in person many years ago and he tells the story with such vividness that I remember it to this day.

They take the baby elephant and tie a chain around its leg. The chain is attached to a heavy spike that is driven into the ground. The baby elephant will try and escape. It will cry mournfully and pull on the spike again and again but eventually it realizes that it is impossible to escape and will no longer waste effort trying to pull away from the stake in the ground.

Then the handler can take the elephant anywhere and can just attach a thin rope and a stick into the ground and the elephant will no longer try to escape. Since it has learned helplessness, it does not believe that it could easily pull the stick out and walk away.

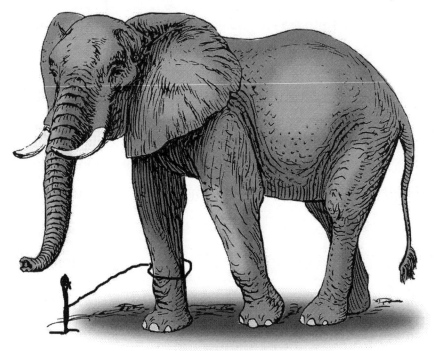

Learned helplessness.

Are you going to believe the lies?

"Nothing is riskier than picking stocks."

"It's too complicated."

"I'm not good with numbers."

"I'm not good with money."

"It's too risky."

Those are all lies. Lies to yourself. Stop lying to yourself. Humans are not one-dimensional beings. We all have multiple talents. Of course, you have a talent in one area that may outshine the others. But almost anybody can do well by investing with their eyes open.

Sadly, many Canadians will still refuse to even start. You can give them this book and they will say they will read it; but they won't. They will find a reason not to. Don't waste time trying to convince others; it is hard enough to convince yourself! The easiest way to convince others is to get rich yourself first and *then* give them this book!

Pull the stake out of the ground and save up that initial $10,000. Find a company that you believe in and learn what they are doing. Stay away from penny-stock promoters. Don't get caught by the pump-and-dump schemes. Find companies that are producing real products. Even if you take your money and invest in the major Canadian banks, you will do far better that any GIC and better than almost any mutual fund.

You may be reading this a few years from the publication date, but the underlying principles will still be relevant.

Yes, the current cannabis green-rush is an easy tidal wave of money that you can surf but there will be others. Some of the biggest opportunities will be in new medical advances that nobody knows about yet. There will always be new opportunities that will reward Canadian investors. Canadians are smart innovators; there will always be new companies that will need to raise money by issuing shares.

The best way to be a 'contrarian' is by not purchasing a new vehicle. Instead make those same bi-weekly or monthly payments into your TFSA. This single decision will alter your financial future in ways that you may have never hoped or dreamed. Who really needs to drive an Escalade? Seriously; and the Ford-150? It keeps getting bigger every year. Then there is the insurance and the gas. Buying a new vehicle is the number one barrier to getting rich in this country. I cannot think of anything that is more stifling to your financial future.

Follow the truth; and the truth is that anyone can become wealthy by diligently saving and investing for themselves. Not saving to purchase a new vehicle and certainly not by saving and handing over your money to someone else to manage for you. Point made, on to the next chapter.

Chapter 10 – Money in the Bank

What if you are morally opposed to investing in Cannabis stocks? This is likely a very real barrier for many Canadians. We are currently experiencing a massive change in the way people view this peculiar plant. Many years from now we may look at the legalization of marijuana as a quaint struggle from the 'olden days' just as we look at the prohibition of alcohol in the 1920's from todays' perspective.

If you are against this sector for whatever reason, there is no need to feel that you have missed out. There are still many opportunities besides the cannabis sector that can provide healthy returns within your TFSA.

Maybe you want a more secure return like a Guaranteed Investment Certificate? A GIC will currently pay between one and two percent interest.

Instead of buying a GIC, why not buy the shares of the banks within your TFSA? Look at the dividends that the banks are currently paying:

CIBC: 4.79 %

Royal Bank: 3.88 %

TD Bank: 3.36 %

Scotia Bank: 4.04 %

Why would you buy a GIC that locks your money in for a year or longer in exchange for 1.5% interest, when you can buy stock in the bank itself and earn any of the above rates? (The rates fluctuate with the price of the underlying stock; as the share price increases, the dividend returns drop and vice versa. If you buy the stock and the price of the stock increases, you gain on the price of the stock but the dividend yield as a percentage of the stock price will drop. You gain on one end and gain less on the other end.)

You are not locked in. You can earn that dividend within your TFSA. And, you have access to your original investment at any time by simply selling your shares. Of course, you will not be paid the dividend if you sell too soon. You may also benefit from capital appreciation of the stock itself. True, the underlying bank stock may drop, but there is always that risk.

There is rarely ever a good reason to buy a GIC. Those that do are in the same condition as that poor elephant pictured above. Unless they have someone take them by the hand and show them. Look, you are free. You are free to invest in stocks. There is no big boogey-man that is going to come out of the closet and eat your money if you invest in the stock market. On the contrary, you will likely make some significant returns on your investment.

As I watch my TFSA balance soar pass the $100,000 mark; after having started with only $10,000, I realize that a lot of the information out there is misleading and turning Canadians into helpless baby elephants. I refuse to be one them; I have pulled the stick out the ground and I am free.

Ask yourself how much time you spend wasting on any unproductive habits. Playing video games? Facebooking? Reading pulp fiction? If you dedicate just thirty minutes per day to the study of finance; how soon would it be before you are a knowledgeable investor? It would not take long at all.

What if you don't like the bank stocks? What other investments are available to you as an investor?

Enbridge Gas (Ticker symbol: ENB) Almost half of Canadian households heat their home using natural gas. This stock is currently yielding a 5% return as a dividend payout to its shareholders. The stock is trading at $48 per share and pays a dividend of $2.44 per share. (2.44 / $48 = 5.03%)

If you are holding the shares prior to the ex-dividend date, you will be paid the dividend for each share you own. If you were to hold $5000 worth of shares, you would earn a dividend of just over $250, paid cash into your TFSA. To calculate the dividend: $5000 / $48 = 104 shares. 104 x $2.44 per share = $254.16

If you held $10,000 worth of shares you would earn over $500 per annum from the dividend payout. That is multiple times better than any GIC.

Brookfield Asset Management (Ticker Symbol:BAM.PF.F)

This company is huge conglomerate with over $250 billion in assets. They currently pay a dividend of $4.50% on their preferred class A shares.

Emera (Ticker Symbol: EMA)

This multi-billion-dollar energy and services company based in Halifax pays a dividend of 4.4%

Fortis Inc (Ticker Symbol: FTS)

This is an Electric Utilities company that currently pays a dividend of 3.5% to its' shareholders. Remember when you played Monopoly as a kid and the Utilities would always pay out a dividend? Things haven't changed, it's still good to own the utilities!

Manulife Financial (Ticker Symbol: MFC)

This multinational insurance company is currently paying a dividend of just under 3.5%.

All the above-mentioned shares may be purchased within your TFSA and will provide you with passive dividend income. Passive income is income that you earn while sleeping! When you have assets working for you, you are earning passive income. This type of income is what will move you from working by the 'sweat of your brow' to have your money make money for you. This is how the wealthy earn income; this is how you should be earning income for yourself and for your children.

Remember the concept of compound returns. If you invest $10,000 into Enbridge gas shares, the first year your account will earn $500 but the second year, you will earn ($10,500 x 5%) = $525. Interest on interest. A million dollars invested in Enbridge stock will pay you $50,000 per year in dividend income. Not too shabby and yes, I could live on that. Eventually someone will build their TFSA to one million dollars; why not you?

Let's imagine you are age 25 and deposit $10,000 into your TFSA and invest it all into Enbridge Gas shares and for this example, we will assume that Enbridge is able to maintain that dividend each year.

Some companies pay a dividend annually and some provide a payout every quarter or every month. That of course depends on the profitability of the company. Some companies pride themselves on having a long history of consistent dividend payouts. Others fluctuate as does the underlying share price. By spending a bit of time studying these and other dividend paying companies, you can learn how to build a portfolio of income producing assets for yourself. Building wealth within your TFSA can be an enjoyable and profitable pastime.

As the share price fluctuates so does the dividend yield. As the share price rises, the dividend yield drops and vice versa. As the share price drops, the dividend yield rises. You can choose when to buy and when to sell depending on the yield. This strategy is much better than 'money in the bank' that would only pay you only a fraction of one percent in interest.

Chapter 11 – The First Ten Thousand

I have mentioned a few times that it is good to start with an initial ten thousand dollars. But what if you don't have that first ten thousand? That is a good question because that is really the most difficult part in turning your TFSA into a million-dollar income generating machine.

Perhaps it will help if I share with you how I saved up my first ten thousand. My income as a writer last year was a little over $13,000. You could say I fit the description as a struggling writer or a starving artist. I did not even make minimum wage. Previous years were not much different.

What I did was make a commitment to consistently deposit ten percent of every penny I earned into my TFSA account. In January of 2016 I reached $10,000 in savings. At that point, I stopped contributing. In November of 2017, my TFSA account passed the $100,000-dollar mark. Twenty-three months. It took me almost three years to save up that first ten-thousand, but it took less than two years to grow that ten-thousand into one-hundred thousand. How long will it take me to go from 100,000 to 1 million?

Getting to one million is still the goal for me and that is partly the reason why I titled this book the million-dollar TFSA. I imagine that someone will hit that mark long before I do, but hit it they will. And when they do, they will have done something that is powerful for themselves and for their loved ones. They will have broken free from the oppressive burden of taxation. This is something that has never been possible before.

Why not you? You have heard the phrase, "You cannot avoid death and taxes." Death, yes; but taxes no more. I expect that the Canadian government may soon limit the amount you can deposit into a TFSA. They may even cap the deposits altogether for fear of letting too many Canadians except the tax trap. We currently have a rare opportunity that did not exist for previous generations. Unless of course you go back prior to 1917 when there was no income tax.[8] . Take advantage of the TFSA program now while you still can; start saving today! If I was able to save up $10,000 on my meager income than so can you!

Someone reading this may state, "Well that is fine for you; you got started early." That is a bad excuse. It's never too late. I would expdect that the best opportunities are still to come. There will be new technologies, new medical breakthroughs and new companies that will take advantage of these new discoveries. When these things happen, often they will need to raise money through the stock-market just as they have done since long before you and I were born.

The first ten-thousand dollars is the most difficult to save because it will force you to change your mindset. You will have to shift from thinking of spending now to thinking of building a future. There are many opponents to this way of thinking. They bombard you every day with images of luxury, of satisfaction, of sunny days now. They spend millions of dollars on advertising in many different formats to get you to spend your money now!

There are no commercials that tell you to invest on your own.

"No money down. Only $96.15 per week for 24 months and you will have your first ten thousand."

"Only $192.30 Bi-weekly Payments on a two year term gets you a chip in the game."

$416.66 per month for 24 months and this shiny new TFSA can be yours."

All the above savings plan amounts will result in a savings of $10,000. You can do the math and see for yourself. Choose a deposit plan and then stick with it like your life depends on it. Because your financial life does depend on it!

Wouldn't it be great if these ads were reminding you to build your TFSA instead of encouraging you to buy a depreciating vehicle? But of course that's not what we hear. We see the ads from the automotive industry. We see all the commercials out there that encourage us to buy fast-food, alcohol and clothing among many other things. Everyone wants you to spend your money but nobody wants you to save it.

Kudos to the Canadian government for having the TFSA program in the first place. Don't be like the thousands of Canadians who open a TFSA and then don't contribute to it. Or worse, that close it at the first sign of a new expense. Start now to commit to building that first ten thousand. You can do it. If I did it while earning less than minimum wage, then so can you.

Building your first ten-thousand requires you to pay yourself first. This concept is not new; it is mentioned in many popular financial books such as, "The Richest Man in Babylon", "The Wealthy Barber" and others. It requires dedication and a kind of, what you might call, a seriousness towards your own financial life. Most people do not take their financial life seriously. They scoff at the idea of becoming wealthy. Don't be a scoffer; be a doer and a saver. Every dollar you save is like a miniature soldier that will work tirelessly to earn you income forever; as long as you allow it. Every dollar you spend is gone forever. Think of your dollars as financial soldiers that will win the war against poverty for you.

What would convince you to start setting aside ten percent of every penny you make into your TFSA? If your life depended on it, would you do it? The fact is that your financial life does depend on it. You have to begin and diligenty set aside starting today. Nobody else is going to do it for you.

How is your TFSA growing today? Has it reached a million dollars yet? If so, please let me know as I would like to be the first to congratulate you on a financial life well played! Keep saving and buidling your future; I wish you good success in all areas of life.

Afterword

The ball is now in your court. Are you going to be one of the first Canadians to build their TFSA up to one million dollars in value? Some surely will, and some may have already done so. Join them by finding companies that are succeeding in their chosen field. You can partner with those companies by being a 'buy-and-hold shareholder." I hope this book has ignited a spark in your motivation. We are all in this boat together. Let's help each other up to a higher level of living and a higher level of success that benefits ourselves, our neighbors and our country!

I pray you have good success in all your investing efforts.
Sincerely,

Patrick Doucette

Notes

[1] My earnings within my TFSA for the month of July 2017

[2] Population Stats are from public data posted by Statistics Canada.
www.statcan.gc.ca

[3] If you are unsure of whether you can withdraw or not, Royal Bank has examples and details that you can check at
https://www.rbcadvicecentre.com/the-rules-for-withdrawing-from-your-tfsa

[4] Data from BMO Financial TFSA Study – Feb. 2017

[5] My TFSA reached $107,000 on November 27, 2017

[6] Ecclesiastes Chapter 4 verse 12

[7] Ecclesiastes Chapter 11 verse 2

[8] Personal income tax was started in Canada in 1917. It was originally supposed to be a temporary tax to help support the war effort during the first world war. If you were married and had an income below $2000 per year, you were exempt from filing taxes. Also, if you were single and had an income below $1000, you were exempt as well. Others who exempt from filing taxes included the Governor General, foreign diplomats and those were in active service overseas. If you did not fall into any of those categories, then filing and paying taxes was mandatory under the *Income War Tax Act of 1917*. If you refused to pay taxes, you could be fined $100 per day up to a maximum penalty of $10,000! That was a severe penalty when one considers that at that time, a married person with an income of $3000 was only obligated to pay $20 in income tax.

Manufactured by Amazon.ca
Bolton, ON

15129351R00051